CW00551848

ISBN 978-0-331-59187-3
PIBN 10546749

LIST OF SUBSCRIBERS.

His Majesty's Libraries, London and Kew.
His Royal Highness the Prince of Wales.
His Royal Highness the Duke of Clarence.
Her Royal Highness the Princess Elizabeth.

A.

Atholl, the Duke of
Almeida, his Excellency the Chevalier
Ainslie, Lord Charles
Apsley, Captain
Arnold, Dr.
Arthur, J. Esq. 2 Copies
Adam, J. W. Esq.
Archer, Edward, Esq.
Ablett,—— Esq.
Arch, Messrs, 3 Copies
Atkinson, Jasper, Esq.
Alexander, Mr. J.
Amyand, ——, Esq.
Akers, ——, Esq.
Arteria, Mr. 6 Copies.
Alexander, Mr. T.
Ackerman, Mr.
Atkins, Mr.

B.

Buccleugh, the Dutchess of
Beauclerk, Lady D.
Blandford, the Marquis of
Bath, the Marquis of
Bathurst, the Earl of
Brooke, Lady
Bayntun, Lady
Buck, Lady
Berry, Sir Edward
Benson, General
Burrard, General
Blomfield, Colonel
Barrow, J. Esq.
Bidwell, J. Esq.
Boydell, Messrs

Bindley, ——, Esq.
Bathurst, Rev. Charles
Beckford, W. Esq.
Braithwaite, Daniel, Esq.
Brand, W. Esq.
Budgen, ——, Esq.
Boys, W. Esq.
Bromley, Rev. M.
Barnard, F. Esq.
Barnard, B. Esq.
Barclay, R. Esq.
Barvis, Jackson, Esq.
Byrne, W. Esq.
Bradney, J. Esq.
Bristol, the Library.
Barker, Mrs.
Bulmer, W. Esq.
Beaumont, —— Esq.
Barnes, Rev. H.
Bick, Edmund, Esq.
Baker, G. Esq.
Bannister, J. Esq.
Bishop, Mr.
Braithwaite, Mr.
Booth, Mr.
Blackmore, Mr.
Binns, Mr. 2 Copies.
Bury, Mr.
Bush, Mr.
Blades, Mr.
Byfield and Hawkesworth, Messrs.
Bell and Bradfute, Messrs, 3 Copies.
Becket, Mr. T.

C.

LIST OF SUBSCRIBERS.

Carpenter, Richard, Esq.
Cowper, C. Esq.
Curtein, E. L. Esq.
Ca——,——, Esq.
Caley,——, Esq.
Ch—— , Jn , Esq.
Charnock, J. Esq.
Cruikshank, W. Esq.
Chy——, Qy   Esq.
Clarke, J. Esq
Clark, Richard, Mr.
Ca , W. Mr.
Gr——   Mr.
Cl——   and Davies, Messrs.
Colnaghi, Me   rs.
Clay and Scriven, Messrs.
Cas   Mr.
Cqr——   Mr.

D.

Dundas, Lord
Douglas, Lady
Daniel, Thomas, Esq.
Dalrymple, Colonel
Dnb——
Dea——,——, Esq.
Dickens,——, Esq.
Dove, H. Esq.
Dorrington, John, Esq.
Dickenson,——, Esq.
Duppa, Richard, Esq.
Deacon, Jas   Esq.
Dundas,——, Esq.
Dowdewell, Jhs
Derrick,——,——, Esq.
Dou e, F. Esq.
Davis,——, Esq.
Deighton, Mr. 6 Copies.

E.

Essex, Earl of
Egremont, Earl of
Englefield, Sir H. C.
Edwards, B. Esq.
Ellis, C. R. Esq.
Erving, G. Esq.
Edridge, W. Esq.
Edridg , H. Esq.
Eagleton,——, Esq.
Elliott, J. Esq.
Edmonds, William, Esq.
Elger, W. Esq.
Ems   John, Esq.
Edwards, Mr.
Evans, Mr.
Edmonds, Mr.
Eccle , Mr.

Ellis, Mr.
Egerton, Mr.

F.

Fitzwilliam, Earl of
Franklin, Governor
Foster, Richard, B q.
Fitzhugh, W. Esq.
Flg   Thomas, Esq.
Faulkener, Rev. Mr.
Fellowes, Robert, Esq.
Forster, Thomas, Esq
Foster, Dr.
Fonnereau, Esq.
Frances, Rev. Ch
Fpo   G. T. H. Esq.
Fearnside, Esq
Ford,——, Esq.
Faden, Mr. 7 Cp i

G.

Grantham, Lady
Greville, the Honourable R. F.
Gower, Admiral Sir Erasmus
Gold, Captain
Gardner, Henry, Esq.
Gostling, G. Esq.
Gordon, Alexander, Esq.
Gordon,——, Esq.
Gebhardt,——, Esq.
Gardner, Thomas, Esq.
Gregory, R. Esq.
Geisweiler, Mr. 2 Copies.

H.

Hackerton, Visc   1
Harcourt, the Honourable General
Harpur, Sir H.
Hoare, Sir Richard Clt
Hpr   Chi   Esq.
Hallam, Chl
Holland, Esq.
Hargrave, Captain
Hyy   Captain
Harman, J. Esq. 2 Copies,
Hgh——   Ozias, Esq.
Haliburton,——, Esq.
Hpa   T. Esq.
Hyl   John, Esq. 2 Cpi .
Hay, T. Esq
Hollingworth, F. Esq.
Harrison, G. Esq.
Homy, E. Esq.
Hughes, Mr. R.
Hughes, Mr.'
Haggard, Mr.
Heidinger, Mr.

Howlett, Mr. B.

I.

Irby, the Honorable W. H.
Johnes, Colonel
Jourdan, Major
Ibbetson, ——, Esq.
Jackson, W. Esq.
Johnstone, Esq.
Josi, C. Esq.
Jenyns Rev. G.
Johnstone, Dr.
Jeffery, Mr.
Jones, Mr.
Jefferies, Mr. 3 Copies.

K.

Kerry, Earl of
Kerr, Lord Mark
Knight, W. Esq.
Kershaw, T. Esq.

L.

Lucas, Lady
Lascelles, Honorable Mr.
Lloyd, Brigadier General
Long, Rev. William
Locker, E. H. Esq.
Locker, J. Esq.
Lynch, P. Esq.
Long, W. Esq.
Laporte, J. Esq.
Landseer, Mr. J.
Le Mesurier, Rev. Thomas.
Lowry, Mr. W.
Lamprey, Mr. S.
Law, Mr.
Lowe, Mr.
Leigh and Sotheby, Messrs.

M.

Macartney, Earl
Macclesfield, the Earl of
Malmesbury, Lord
Millman, Sir Francis
Morshead, Sir John
Musgrave, Sir John
Macleod, Colonel
Maclean, Captain
Maxwell, Atcheson, Esq.
Maynard, Thomas, Esq.

Mathison, ——, Esq. 2 Copies.
Magniac, ——, Esq.
Meyler, ——, Esq.
Medland, T. Mr.
Morrison, Mr. ——,
Mascall, Mr.
Martin, Mr.
Manners and Miller, Messrs.
Meyer, Mr.

N.

Nicolai, F. Esq.
Newberry, Francis, Esq.
Nash, ——, Esq.

O.

Ossory, Earl of Upper
Ommaney, Captain.
Ommaney, F. M. Esq.
O'Brien, Captain.
Oakley, B. Esq.

P.

Pembroke, the Countess of
Peachey, John, Esq.
Parish, Captain.
Phipps, Captain.
Pennant, Thomas, Esq.
Parker, Mrs. C.
Pollock, William, Esq.
Pigou, ——, Esq.
Palmer, J. S. Esq.
Parish, W. Esq.
Power, ——, Esq.
Pankhurst, ——, Esq.
Power, Mr. Alexander.
Powel, Rev. G.
Petre, Mrs. John.
Phillips, Mr.
Parker, Eliz, and Co.
Powel, Mr. J.
Payne, Mr.
Pouncy, Mr.

R.

Roxburgh, the Duke of
Rushout, the Honorable Miss
Rainsford, General
Ramsey, Colonel
Roupell, G. B. Esq.
Ranking, G. Esq.

PORTRAIT OF VAN-TA-ZHIN,

A military Mandarine (or Nobleman) of China.

THIS officer (a colleague of Chow-ta-zhin, who was a mandarine of the civil department) was appointed by the Emperor to attend the British Embassy, from the time of its arrival in the gulf of Pe-tchi-li, till its departure from Canton. Van-ta-zhin was a man of a bold, generous, and amiable character, and possessed of qualifications eminently suited to his profession, being well skilled in the use of the bow, and in the management of the sabre. For services performed in the wars of Thibet, he wore appended from his cap, a peacock's feather, as an extraordinary mark of favour from his sovereign, besides a red globe of coral which distinguished his rank. He is represented in his usual, or undress, consisting of a short loose jacket of fine cotton, and an under vest of embroidered silk; from his girdle hang suspended his handkerchief, his knife and chopsticks* in a case, and purses for tobacco: on his thumbs are two broad rings of agate, for the purpose of drawing the bowstring. The heads of the arrows, which are thrust into the quiver, are variously pointed, as barbed, lozenge-headed, &c. His boots are of satin, with thick soles of paper: these are always worn by the mandarines and superior Chinese.

* Quoit-zau, or Chopsticks, are used in China instead of forks; they are two round slender sticks of ivory, ebony, &c. and used in the manner of pincers.

London Published July 26, 1797, by G. Nicol, Pall mall.

M. Rosenberg fecit.

A P E A S A N T,

With his Wife and Family.

SMOKING tobacco is so universally prevalent in China, that it is not
unusual to see girls of only twelve years of age enjoying this recreation.
The Mother is in the dress of the northern provinces; the peak on her
forehead is of velvet, and adorned with a bead of agate or glass, The
hair is combed back so smooth by the assistance of oil, that it more
resembles japan than hair; on the back of her head is a loop of leather,
and the whole is kept together by bodkins of ivory or tortoise-shell.
The general dress of this class of people, male or female, is nankeen
dyed of various colours, though blue or black is most commonly
worn.

The usual method of carrying infants, by mothers who are employed
in any manufacture, or at any manual labour, as sculling of boats, &c.
is by attaching them to the back in a kind of bag.   Sometimes two
children are seen fastened at the shoulders in the same manner.   The
Father wears appended from his girdle, a tobacco purse, knife case,
and his flint and steel, by which the Chinese light a pipe very expe-
ditiously. The elder Girl has her hair twisted into a hard knob at the
crown, and ornamented with artificial flowers; she is prepared for
dinner, having her bowl of rice by her, and her chopsticks in her
hand.   The feet of children are prevented from growing larger, by
hard bandages bound strongly round them, the four smaller toes are
turned under the foot, closely compressed, and the great toe forms the
point.   In consequence of this extraordinary custom the feet of adult
women seldom exceed five inches and a half; even the peasantry pique
themselves on the smallness of their feet, and take great care to adorn
them with embroidered silk shoes, and bands for the ankles, while the
rest of their habiliments display the most abject poverty.

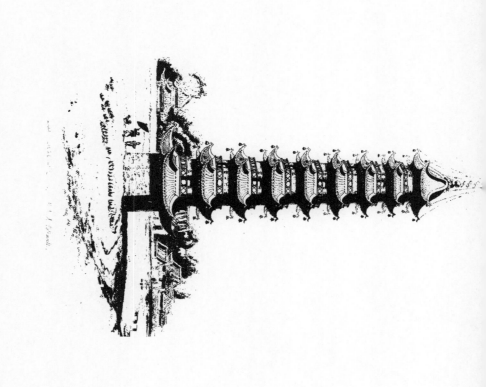

A PAGODA (OR TOWER)

Near the City of Sou-tcheou.

THESE buildings are a striking feature on the face of the country.
The Chinese name for them is Ta; but Europeans have improperly
denominated them Pagodas, a term used in some Oriental countries
for a temple of religious worship. It seems the Ta of China is not
intended for sacred purposes, but erected occasionally by viceroys or
rich mandarines, either for the gratification of personal vanity, or with
the idea of transmitting a name to posterity ; or perhaps built by the
magistracy merely as objects to enrich the landscape.

They are generally built of brick, and sometimes cased with porcelain, and chiefly consist of nine, though some have only seven or
five stories, each having a gallery, which may be entered from the
windows, and a projecting roof, covered with tiles of a rich yellow
colour, highly glazed, which receive from the sun a splendour equal
to burnished gold. At each angle of the roofs a light bell is suspended,
which is rung by the force of the wind, and produces a jingling not
altogether unpleasant. These buildings are for the most part octagonal,
though some few are hexagonal, and round. They diminish gradually
in circumference from the foundation to the summit, and have a stair-
case within, by which they ascend to the upper story. In height they
are generally from an hundred to an hundred and fifty feet, and are
situated indiscriminately on eminences or plains, or oftener in cities.
The Print represents one of modern structure. Those of a more
ancient date are in a mutilated state, and the roofs covered with grey
tiles, overgrown with moss, while others have a cornice only instead
of the projecting roof.

Vide the print of Lin-tsin Pagoda in Sir George Staunton's Account
of the Chinese Embassy.

occupied by the proprietor; the fore part of the vessel by his servants, and the aft or stern part is used for culinary purposes, and sleeping places for the boatmen. Barges of this kind have one large sail of matting, stretched out by bamboos, running horizontally across it; the sail may be instantly taken in by letting go the haulyards, when the sail falls in folds similar to a fan. When the wind or tide is unfavourable, these vessels are either tracked along by human labour, or sculled by large oars which work on pivots at the bows and stern: by means of these oars, which are never taken out of the water, but simply sculled to and fro, the vessel is impelled onwards with considerable rapidity. The triple umbrella proclaims a Mandarine of consequence to be on board. The large lanterns with Chinese characters on them, and the ensign at the stern, are likewise marks of distinction.

THE TRAVELLING BARGE

Of Van-ta-zhin.

As travelling in China is generally performed on the water, a prodigious number of Yachts or Barges of various forms are employed, as well for that purpose, as for the conveyance of merchandize.

The central apartment, which has an awning over the windows, is occupied by the proprietor; the fore part of the vessel by his servants, and the aft or stern part is used for culinary purposes, and sleeping places for the boatmen. Barges of this kind have one large sail of matting, stretched out by bamboos, running horizontally across it; the sail may be instantly taken in by letting go the haulyards, when the sail falls in folds similar to a fan. When the wind or tide is unfavourable, these vessels are either tracked along by human labour, or sculled by large oars which work on pivots at the bows and stern: by means of these oars, which are never taken out of the water, but simply sculled to and fro, the vessel is impelled onwards with considerable rapidity. The triple umbrella proclaims a Mandarine of consequence to be on board. The large lanterns with Chinese characters on them, and the ensign at the stern, are likewise marks of distinction.

A CHINESE SOLDIER OF INFANTRY,

Or Tiger of War.

THE dress of the Chinese is generally loose ; the soldiers of this part of the army, with few exceptions, are the only natives whose close habit discovers the formation of the limbs.

The general uniform of the Chinese troops is cumbrous and inconvenient; this of the Tiger of War, is much better adapted for military action.

The Missionaries have denominated them TIGERS of War, from their dress, which has some resemblance to that animal; being striped, and having ears on the cap.

They are armed with a scimitar of rude workmanship, and a shield of wicker or basket-work, so well manufactured, as to resist the heaviest blow from a sword. On it is painted the face of an imaginary monster, which (like that of Medusa) is supposed to possess the power of petrifying the beholder.

At a distance is seen a Military Post, with the Imperial flag, which is yellow, hoisted near it.

A GROUP OF TRACKERS

Of the Vessels, at Dinner.

W H E N the wind or tide is unfavourable to the progress of the vessels, the sail and oars are laid aside, and the more general mode of tracking them is adopted. The number of trackers employed, depends on the size of the vessel, or strength of the current, which often requires the efforts of twenty men to counteract: these are kept in full exertion by a task-master, who most liberally applies the whip, where he sees a disposition to idleness.

The chief food of these poor labourers, is rice; and they consider it a luxury, when they can procure vegetables fried in rancid oil, or animal offal, to mix with it. They are represented cooking their meal over an earthen stove; the standing figure is employed eating his rice in the usual way, which is by placing the edge of the bowl against his lower lip, and with the chopsticks knocking the contents into his mouth.

They sometimes wear shoes made of straw, but are more frequently without any. The pien-za, or queue, is often inconvenient to Chinese labourers; to avoid which they twist it round their heads, and secure it by tucking in its extremity.

The flat boards, with cordage to them, are applied to the breast when dragging the junks, or vessels.

VIEW OF A BRIDGE,

In the Environs of the City of Sou-tcheou.

THE Bridges of China are variously constructed. There are many of three arches, some of which are very light, and elegant; others are simply pyramidal piers, with timbers and flooring laid horizontally across them.

This arch, which resembles the outline of a horseshoe, occurred very frequently in the route of a part of the Embassy from Han-tcheou to Chusan. Like most of the Chinese bridges, it is of quick ascent, making an angle of full twenty degrees with the horizon, and is ascended by steps. The carriage of merchandize by land, is therefore inconsiderable; the rivers and canals being the high roads of China.

The material of which these bridges are composed, is a species of coarse marble. The projecting stones and uprights against the surface, are supposed to strengthen or bind the fabric; and the five circular badges over the arch, contain Chinese characters, which may probably shew the name of the architect, and date of its erection.

The temporary ornament over the centre of the arch, consisting of upright poles, painted and adorned with silken streamers, and suspended lanterns, was erected in compliment to the Embassador. The six soldiers from an adjacent Military Post, were likewise ordered to stand on the bridge, by way of salute.

London Published Oct 10, 1821 by R.A. Alexander

PORTRAIT OF A TRADING SHIP

These ships venture as far as Manilla, Japan, and even Batavia, which is the most distant port they visit; and many of them are from eight hundred to a thousand tons burthen. In these voyages the mariners take the moderate season of the year, and though well acquainted with the use of the compass, generally keep near the coast.

No alteration has been made in the naval architecture of China for many centuries past. The Chinese are so averse to innovation, and so attached to ancient prejudices, that although Canton is annually frequented by the ships of various European nations, whose superiority of construction they must acknowledge, yet they reject any improvement in their vessels.

The stern of this ship falls in with an angle; other vessels are formed with a cavity, in which the rudder is defended from the violence of the sea; yet this contrivance certainly subjects the ship to much hazard, when running before the wind in high seas.

On each bow is painted an eye, with the pupil turned forwards; perhaps with the idea of keeping up some resemblance to a fish; or from

PORTRAIT OF A TRADING SHIP.

THESE ships venture as far as Manilla, Japan, and even Batavia, which is the most distant port they visit; and many of them are from eight hundred to a thousand tons burthen. In these voyages the mariners take the moderate season of the year, and though well acquainted with the use of the compass, generally keep near the coast.

No alteration has been made in the naval architecture of China for many centuries past. The Chinese are so averse to innovation, and so attached to ancient prejudices, that although Canton is annually frequented by the ships of various European nations, whose superiority of construction they must acknowledge, yet they reject any improvement in their vessels.

The stern of this ship falls in with an angle; other vessels are formed with a cavity, in which the rudder is defended from the violence of the sea; yet this contrivance certainly subjects the ship to much hazard, when running before the wind in high seas.

On each bow is painted an eye, with the pupil turned forwards; perhaps with the idea of keeping up some resemblance to a fish; or from a superstitious notion, that the ship may thus see before her, and avoid danger.

The ports often serve as windows, not many of them being furnished with ordnance.

same material, dyed of another colour, sewed into it at equal
and has a collar of sable, or fox skin. This surtout is wor
mornings and evenings as are fresh and cold; in the day time (i
conveniently hot) it is laid aside. Under this is worn a vest
silk; beneath which is another of white linen, or taffeta; and la
of loose drawers: in the summer season these are of linen or si
the winter, they are lined with fur, or quilted with raw silk;
northern provinces they are worn, made of skins only.

The cap is composed of a coarse sort of felt, which is very
and while new, they have the shape of those worn by the Man
the Portrait of Van-ta-zhin), but they soon become pliant and
by wear, or when rain has taken the stiffness from them. Th
are of nankeen, quilted on the inside with cotton. The shoes
nankeen, with thick soles made of paper.

From the girdle on the right side, hangs a flint and steel,
sheath; on the left, purses for tobacco, or snuff.

The box held in his hand contains sweetmeats; a jar of wh

PORTRAIT OF THE PURVEYOR

For the Embassy, while the Embassador remained at Macao.

The dress of this figure is the same as is generally worn by the citizens, or middle class of people in China, with variations in the colour; and some difference of form in hats, caps, boots, &c. &c.

The external jacket is of sheep skin, ornamented with crescents of the same material, dyed of another colour, sewed into it at equal distances; and has a collar of sable, or fox skin. This surtout is worn on such mornings and evenings as are fresh and cold; in the day time (if found inconveniently hot) it is laid aside. Under this is worn a vest of figured silk; beneath which is another of white linen, or taffeta; and lastly, a pair of loose drawers: in the summer season these are of linen or silk, and for the winter, they are lined with fur, or quilted with raw silk; and in the northern provinces they are worn, made of skins only.

The cap is composed of a coarse sort of felt, which is very common; and while new, they have the shape of those worn by the Mandarins, (see the Portrait of Van-ta-zhin), but they soon become pliant and misshapen, by wear, or when rain has taken the stiffness from them. The stockings are of nankeen, quilted on the inside with cotton. The shoes are likewise nankeen, with thick soles made of paper.

From the girdle on the right side, hangs a flint and steel, and knife sheath; on the left, purses for tobacco, or snuff.

The box held in his hand contains sweetmeats; a jar of which he entreated the persons of the Embassy to accept as a token of his regard.

The back ground, is a scene at Macao.

other holes, for the hands of the delinquent, who is sometimes so far favoured as to have but one hand confined; by which indulgence he is enabled with the other to lessen the weight on his shoulders.

The division in the Cangue which receives the head, is kept together by pegs, and is further secured by a slip of paper pasted over the joint, on which is affixed the seal, or chop, of the Mandarin; and the cause of punishment likewise depicted on it, in large characters.

The weight of these ignominious machines, which are from sixty to two hundred pounds in weight, and the time criminals are sentenced to endure them, depends on the magnitude of the offence, being sometimes extended, without intermission, to the space of one, two, or even three months; during which time the offender's nights are spent in the prison, and in the morning he is brought by the magistrates' assistant, led by a chain, to a gate of the city, or any place most frequented; when the attendant suffers him to rest his burthen against a wall, where he remains ex-

PUNISHMENT OF THE CANGUE.

By which name it is commonly known to Europeans, but by the Chinese called the Tcha; being a heavy tablet, or collar of wood, with a hole through the centre, or rather two pieces of wood hollowed in the middle which inclose the neck (similar to our pillory), there are, likewise, two other holes, for the hands of the delinquent, who is sometimes so far favoured as to have but one hand confined; by which indulgence he is enabled with the other to lessen the weight on his shoulders.

The division in the Cangue which receives the head, is kept together by pegs, and is further secured by a slip of paper pasted over the joint, on which is affixed the seal, or chop, of the Mandarin; and the cause of punishment likewise depicted on it, in large characters.

The weight of these ignominious machines, which are from sixty to two hundred pounds in weight, and the time criminals are sentenced to endure them, depends on the magnitude of the offence, being sometimes extended, without intermission, to the space of one, two, or even three months; during which time the offender's nights are spent in the prison, and in the morning he is brought by the magistrates' assistant, led by a chain, to a gate of the city, or any place most frequented; when the attendant suffers him to rest his burthen against a wall, where he remains exposed throughout the day to the derision of the populace, without the means of taking food but by assistance. Nor is the punishment at an end when the Mandarin has ordered him to be released from the Cangue; a certain number of blows from the bamboo, remain to be inflicted; for which chastisement, in the most abject manner, with forehead to the earth, he thanks the Mandarin for his fatherly correction.

London Publish'd May 1. 1798. by G. Nicol Pall-mall.

SOUTH GATE OF THE CITY OF TING-HAI,

In the Harbour of Chu-san.

The Port of Tchu-san, into which the English were formerly admitted, lies in latitude, thirty degrees and twenty minutes north, or about midway, on the east coast of China, between Can-ton and Pe-king.

The walls inclosing this city are near thirty feet in height, which (excepting Pagodas, public buildings, &c.) entirely preclude the sight of the houses, which in general have but one story.

The bricks and tiles of China, either from a different quality of the substance that composes them, or from being dried and burnt in a different manner, are of a bluish, or slate colour. The embrasures have no artillery, but there are loop-holes in the merlons for the use of archers. On the walls, and at the entrance of the gate, are tents as guard-houses, where a sufficient number of soldiers are continually stationed. At an early hour of the night the gates are shut, after which, no person can be admitted on any pretence whatever.

The angles of the roofs which curve upwards, and project considerably, in Chinese buildings, most likely have their origin from tents; for a canvas resting on four cords would receive the same form. The ridges on the angles of the buildings over the gate are decorated with figures of animals, dragons, &c.; and the sides of the building, and extremities of the beams, painted with various colours. The yellow board over the arch has Chinese characters on it; which probably signify the name and rank of the city. The carriage entering the city, is a vehicle used in common with sedans, for the conveyance of persons of consequence. The Chinese have not adopted the use of springs, therefore these machines are little better than a European cart. The nearest figure shews the usual method of carrying light burthens, as vegetables, fruit, &c. &c.

SOUTH GATE OF THE CITY OF TING-HAI,

In the Harbour of Tchu-san.

THE Port of Tchu-san, into which the English were formerly admitted, lies in latitude, thirty degrees and twenty minutes north, or about midway, on the east coast of China, between Can-ton and Pe-king.

The walls inclosing this city are near thirty feet in height, which (excepting Pagodas, public buildings, &c.) entirely preclude the sight of the houses, which in general have but one story.

The bricks and tiles of China, either from a different quality of the substance that composes them, or from being dried and burnt in a different manner, are of a bluish, or slate colour. The embrasures have no artillery, but there are loop-holes in the merlons for the use of archers. On the walls, and at the entrance of the gate, are tents as guard-houses, where a sufficient number of soldiers are continually stationed. At an early hour of the night the gates are shut, after which, no person can be admitted on any pretence whatever.

The angles of the roofs which curve upwards, and project considerably, in Chinese buildings, most likely have their origin from tents; for a canvas resting on four cords would receive the same form. The ridges on the angles of the buildings over the gate are decorated with figures of animals, dragons, &c.; and the sides of the building, and extremities of the beams, painted with various colours. The yellow board over the arch has Chinese characters on it; which probably signify the name and rank of the city. The carriage entering the city, is a vehicle used in common with sedans, for the conveyance of persons of consequence. The Chinese have not adopted the use of springs, therefore these machines are little better than a European cart. The nearest figure shews the usual method of carrying light burthens, as vegetables, fruit, &c. &c.

THREE VESSELS LYING AT ANCHOR

In the River of Ning-po.

THE middle vessel, with the stern in view, was a trading ship without cargo; in this the peculiar construction of the stern is exemplified, being hollowed into an indented angle, for the protection of the rudder, which is lifted out of the water by a rope, to preserve it. The Chinese characters over the rudder, denote the name of the vessel; and the bisected cone against the stern, is appropriated to the same use as the quarter-galleries of our ships.

The small vessel was hired for the service of the Embassy, and employed in transporting baggage; the larger vessel conveyed a part of the Embassy from Ning-po, to Tchu-san, where they embarked on board the Hindostan, for Can-ton. The prow of this vessel has a singular appearance, the upper part of the stern terminating in two wings, or horns. The small boat (or Sam-paan, as called by the Chinese) is a necessary appendage to vessels of this size.

wear an ornament resembling a cap, exquisitely wrought in wood, &c. which they affix to the back of the head.

This figure is from one of the Lamas inhabiting the temple called Poo-ta-la, which is situated near the Imperial residence at Zhe-hol in Tartary. These Priests are all clad in the royal colour, yellow; their hats have very broad brims, answering the double purpose of defence from sun and rain, and are neatly manufactured from straw and split bamboo.

The temple Poo-ta-la, which is distantly seen, maintains eight hundred Lamas, devoted to the worship of the deity Fo: to this sect the Emperor is attached, and it is the general religion of the empire. The

PORTRAIT OF A LAMA, OR BONZE.

THE priesthood of China and Tartary are, since the conquest of the former, become nearly the same, in respect to manners, dress, &c.; and these are the only people of either nation, who have the head shaved entirely. Their general habit is a loose robe or gown, with a broad collar of silk or velvet; the colour of the robe depending on the particular sect or monastery to which they belong. Some of them wear an ornament resembling a cap, exquisitely wrought in wood, &c. which they affix to the back of the head.

This figure is from one of the Lamas inhabiting the temple called Poo-ta-la, which is situated near the Imperial residence at Zhe-hol in Tartary. These Priests are all clad in the royal colour, yellow; their hats have very broad brims, answering the double purpose of defence from sun and rain, and are neatly manufactured from straw and split bamboo.

The temple Poo-ta-la, which is distantly seen, maintains eight hundred Lamas, devoted to the worship of the deity Fo: to this sect the Emperor is attached, and it is the general religion of the empire. The form of this edifice is square, with lesser buildings in the Chinese style of architecture adjoining: each side of the large building measures two hundred feet, and is nearly of the same height, having eleven rows of windows. In the centre of this immense fabric is a chapel, profusely decorated and roofed with tiles of solid gold. Within this chapel is the sanctum sanctorum, containing statues of the idol Fo, with his wife and child.

THE female sex in China live retired in proportion to their situation in life. The lower orders are not more domesticated than in Europe; but the middle class are not often seen from home, and ladies of rank scarcely ever. Alterations of dress are never made from caprice or fashion; the season of the year, and disposing the various ornaments, making the only difference. Instead of linen, the ladies substitute silk netting; over which is worn an under vest and drawers of taffeta; and, (should the weather require no additional covering,) they have for the external garment, a long robe of silk or satin, richly embroidered. Great care is taken in ornamenting the head: the hair, after being smoothed with oil and closely twisted, is brought to the crown of the head, and fastened with bodkins of gold and silver: across the forehead is a band, from which descends a peak of velvet, decorated with a diamond or pearl, and artificial flowers are fancifully arranged on each side of the head. Ear-rings, and the string of perfumed beads suspended from the shoulder, likewise make up part of the ornaments of dress. The use of cosmetics is well known among the ladies of China; painting the face both white and red, is in common practice with them: they place a decided red spot on the lower lip, and the eyebrows are brought by art to be very narrow, black, and arched.

The small shoes are elegantly wrought, and the contour of the shoes are never seen, by means of the loose bandage round them. Boys, till about seven years of age, frequently have two queues, one on each side, to grow from each side of the head. The servant, as is usual with the

A CHINESE LADY AND HER SON,

attended by a Servant.

THE female sex in China live retired in proportion to their situation in life. The lower orders are not more domesticated than in Europe; but the middle class are not often seen from home, and ladies of rank scarcely ever. Alterations of dress are never made from caprice or fashion; the season of the year, and disposing the various ornaments, making the only difference. Instead of linen, the ladies substitute silk netting; over which is worn an under vest and drawers of taffeta; and, (should the weather require no additional covering,) they have for the external garment, a long robe of silk or satin, richly embroidered. Great care is taken in ornamenting the head: the hair, after being smoothed with oil and closely twisted, is brought to the crown of the head, and fastened with bodkins of gold and silver; across the forehead is a band, from which descends a peak of velvet, decorated with a diamond or pearl, and artificial flowers are fancifully arranged on each side of the head. Ear-rings, and the string of perfumed beads suspended from the shoulder, likewise make up part of the ornaments of dress. The use of cosmetics is well known among the ladies of China; painting the face both white and red, is in common practice with them: they place a decided red spot on the lower lip, and the eyebrows are brought by art to be very narrow, black, and arched.

The small shoes are elegantly wrought, and the contour of the ankles are never seen, by reason of the loose bandage round them. Boys, till about seven years of age, frequently have two queues, encouraged to grow from each side of the head. The servant, as is usual with the lower class, wears on the wrist a ring of brass or tutenag.

VIEW OF A BURYING PLACE.

near Hial-sienamun.

THE tombs and monuments of China exhibit variety of architecture, except those of the common people, which are nothing more than small cones of earth, on the summits of which they frequently plant dwarf trees. These simple graves are occasionally visited by the family, who are particularly careful to trim and keep them in neat order.

The coffins of this country are made of very thick boards, plentifully pitched within, and varnished without; which makes them durable, and prevents them from emitting putrid exhalations: this process being absolutely necessary, where the coffins of the lower class often lie scattered among the tombs, totally uncovered with earth.

The rich spare no expence in having coffins of the most precious wood, which are frequently provided several years before the death of the persons intending to occupy them. A deceased parent is oftentimes preserved in the house by an affectionate family for months, and even years; yet either from their knowledge of embalming, or from the practice of securing the joints of the coffin with bitumen, no contagious effluvia proceeds from it.

The duty of the widow or children is not finished here; even after the corpse is deposited in the sepulchre of its ancestors, the disconsolate relatives (clad in coarse canvas) still reside with the body, and continue their lamentations for some months. The characters on the monuments, signify the name and quality of the defunct; and epitaphs, extolling the virtues of the deceased, are inscribed on tablets of marble at the entrance of the vaults. The tomb with steps before it, and another, inclosed with cypresses, are common with people of affluence.

VIEW OF A BURYING-PLACE,

near Han-tcheou-fou.

The tombs and monuments of China exhibit a variety of architecture, except those of the common people, which are nothing more than small cones of earth, on the summits of which they frequently plant dwarf trees. These simple graves are occasionally visited by the family, who are particularly careful to trim and keep them in neat order.

The coffins of this country are made of very thick boards, plentifully pitched within, and varnished without; which makes them durable, and prevents them from emitting putrid exhalations: this process being absolutely necessary, where the coffins of the lower class often lie scattered among the tombs, totally uncovered with earth.

The rich spare no expence in having coffins of the most precious wood, which are frequently provided several years before the death of the persons intending to occupy them. A deceased parent is oftentimes preserved in the house by an affectionate family for months, and even years; yet, either from their knowledge of embalming, or from the practice of securing the joints of the coffin with bitumen, no contagious effluvia proceeds from it.

The duty of the widow or children is not finished here; even after the corpse is deposited in the sepulchre of its ancestors, the disconsolate relatives (clad in coarse canvas) still reside with the body, and continue their lamentations for some months. The characters on the monuments, signify the name and quality of the defunct; and epitaphs, extolling the virtues of the deceased, are inscribed on tablets of marble at the entrance of the vaults. The tomb with steps before it, and another, inclosed with cypresses, are common with people of affluence.

London Published Jan 1st 1798 by G. Nicol Pall Mall

required for those of greater burthen; in this case, there are holes in ground to receive them. When a boat is ready to pass over, the ropes fi the capstans (which have a loop at their extremities) are brought to the s of the vessel; one loop is then passed through the other, and a bille wood thrust into the noose, to prevent their separation; the projecting g wale at the same time keeping the ropes in a proper situation. This be adjusted, the men heave at the capstans till the boat has passed the equ brium, when, by its own gravity, it is launched with great velocity the lower canal, and is prevented from shipping too much water, b strong skreen of basket-work, which is placed at the head. On the

FRONT VIEW OF A BOAT,

passing over an inclined Plane or Glacis.

IN the passage from Han-tcheou-fou to Tehu-san (which was the route of part of the Embassy), the face of the country is mountainous; therefore the communication of the canals is continued by means of this sort of locks, two of which were passed over on the 16th of November, 1793.

In this subject, the difference of level between the two canals was full six feet; in the higher one, the water was within one foot of the upper edge of the beam over which the boat passes. The machinery consisted of a double glacis of sloping masonry, with an inclination of about forty degrees from the horizon. The boats are drawn over by capstans, two of which are generally sufficient, though sometimes four or six are required for those of greater burthen; in this case, there are holes in the ground to receive them. When a boat is ready to pass over, the ropes from the capstans (which have a loop at their extremities) are brought to the stern of the vessel; one loop is then passed through the other, and a billet of wood thrust into the noose, to prevent their separation; the projecting gun-wale at the same time keeping the ropes in a proper situation. This being adjusted, the men heave at the capstans till the boat has passed the equili-brium, when, by its own gravity, it is launched with great velocity into the lower canal, and is prevented from shipping too much water, by a strong skreen of basket-work, which is placed at the head. On the left hand stands a mutilated triumphal arch, and a small temple inclosing an idol, to which sacrifices are frequently made for the preservation of the vessels passing over.

For a plan and section of the above, vide Sir George Staunton's Account, Plate 34 of the folio volume.

THE empire of China has, since the conquest of the Tartars, enjoyed uninterrupted tranquillity, if we except partial insurrections, &c. and in consequence of this long intermission of service, the Chinese army are become enervated, and want the courage, as well as the discipline, of European troops; for strict order is so little enforced, that it is not uncommon to see many among them fanning themselves while standing in the ranks.

The candidates for promotion, in their army, are required not only to give proofs of their knowledge in military tactics, but they must likewise exhibit trials of personal strength and agility, by shooting at the target, exercising the matchlock, sabre, &c.

The situation of the soldiery is even envied by the lower classes, as they regularly receive their pay, though their services are seldom required, but occasionally to assist in quelling tumults, or doing duty at the military posts; thus, for the greater part of their time, they follow their several occupations, having little else to do than keep their arms and accoutrements bright and in good order, ready for the inspection of the officers, should they be suddenly called out to a review, or any other emergency.

This dress of the troops is clumsy, inconvenient, and inimical to the performance of military exercises, yet a battalion thus equipped has, at some distance, a splendid and even warlike appearance; but on closer inspection these coats of mail are found to be nothing more than quilted nankeen, enriched with thin plates of metal, surrounded with studs, which gives the *tout-ensemble* very much the appearance of armour.

From the crown of the helmet (which is the only part that is iron) issues a spear, inclosed with a tassel of dyed horse-hair. The characters on the breast-plate, denote the corps to which he belongs; and the box which is worn in front, serves to contain heads of arrows, bowstrings, &c. &c. The lower part of the bow is inclosed in a sheath or case.

London Published March 1st 1799 by Cadell Russell.

A GROUP OF PEASANTRY, WATERMEN, &c.

THE Chinese are so much .... to gaming that there are seldom without a pack of cards, or a set .... fortune-telling to be practised among them; and quails are also bred for the same purpose. They have likewise a large species of grasshopper (or cricket, common in China; a couple of these are put into a basin to fight, while the by-standers bet sums of money on the issue of the conflict: these insects assail each other with great animosity, frequently tearing off a limb by the violence of their attacks. The Chinese dice are marked exactly similar to those of Europe; in playing they never use a box, but cast them out of the hand. The laws of the empire allowing them full power to dispose of their wives and children, instances have happened when these have been put to the hazard of a throw; and it should be mentioned, that in all their games, whether for amusement or avarice, the Chinese are very ...... and quarrelsome. The figure standing with an instrument of agriculture in his hand, is an husbandman; another sitting figure, with a small black cap, is a watchman, having by him a gong, which is an instrument of sound not ...... a pot-lid; this being struck with the stick lying near it, produces a harsh jarring sound, which is heard at a considerable distance: one of these is always suspended at the head of every vessel when tracked along the canals, and struck as occasion requires by the people on board, to inform the trackers when to desist and ..... and when to resume their labour. By this method much confusion is prevented, where the great concourse of vessels would be otherwise running foul of each other, if not warned by this contrivance.

These gongs have so ...... tone, that the watchmen know perfectly when the signals ..... from the vessel they are tending.

A GROUP OF PEASANTRY, WATERMEN, &c.

playing with Dice.

THE Chinese are so much addicted to gaming, that they are seldom without a pack of cards, or a set of dice. Cock-fighting is in practice among them; and quails are also bred for the same purpose. They have likewise a large species of grasshopper (or grillæ) common in China; a couple of these are put into a bason to fight, while the by-standers bet sums of money on the issue of the conflict: these insects assail each other with great animosity, frequently tearing off a limb by the violence of their attacks. The Chinese dice are marked exactly similar to those of Europe; in playing they never use a box, but cast them out of the hand. The laws of the empire allowing them full power to dispose of their wives and children, instances have happened when these have been put to the hazard of a throw; and it should be mentioned, that in all their games, whether for amusement or avarice, the Chinese are very noisy and quarrelsome. The figure standing with an instrument of agriculture in his hand, is an husbandman; another sitting figure, with a small black cap, is a waterman, having by him a gong, which is an instrument of semi-metal resembling a pot-lid; this being struck with the stick lying near it, produces a harsh jarring sound, which is heard at a considerable distance: one of these is always suspended at the head of every vessel when tracked along the canals, and struck as occasion requires, by the people on board, to inform the trackers when to desist hauling, and when to resume their labour. By this method much confusion is prevented, where the great concourse of vessels would be continually running foul of each other, if not warned by this contrivance.

These gongs have so many various notes, that the trackers know perfectly when the signal is made from the vessel they are hauling.

London Published March 1st 1799 by G. Nicol Pall mall.

the foundation, which is of stone, and has been undermined, most

VIEW OF A CASTLE,

near the City of Tien-sin.

THIS castle, or tower, is situated on a point of land at the confluence of three rivers, the Pei-ho, the Yun-leang, and the When-ho, near the celestial city (Tien-sin), which is the chief harbour for shipping, and principal depot for merchandize throughout China; and from whence the various articles of commerce are circulated, by means of the canals, through the most distant provinces.

This edifice is thirty-five feet in height, and built with bricks, except the foundation, which is of stone, and has been undermined, most likely by indundation; the surrounding country being very low and marshy. A guard of soldiers is constantly stationed here, and, in cases of tumult or commotion, the centinels give the alarm to the adjacent military posts, in the daytime by hoisting a signal, and at night by the explosion of fireworks; on which the neighbouring garrisons repair to the spot where their services are required.

Within the battlements is a building to shelter centinels on duty; one of them is beating a gong, to announce to the garrison the approach of a viceroy or mandarin of rank; on this notice, they immediately form in a rank, and stand under arms to salute him. Within the parapet a lantern is suspended, and in the opposite angle the imperial standard is elevated; the colour of the tablet, with the inscription on it, likewise shews it to be a royal edifice, In Nieu-hoff's account of the Dutch embassy, which was sent to Pekin in the year 1650, is a print either of this tower, or one similar to it, which stood on the same site. The hillocks of earth under a clump of trees, seen in the distance, are burying-places.

A SEA VESSEL UNDER SAIL.

SHIPS of this construction are employed by the merchants, in conveying the produce of the several provinces to the different ports of the empire.

The hold for the stowage of the various commodities, is divided into several partitions, which are so well caulked, with a composition called chu-nam, as to be water-proof; by this contrivance, in the event of a leak, the greater part of the cargo is preserved from injury, and the danger of foundering considerably removed.

The main and foresails are of matting, strongly interwoven, and extended by spars of bamboo running horizontally across them; the mizen and topsails are nankeen, the latter of which is (contrary to the European method) never hoisted higher than is seen in the drawing. The sails are braced up or eased off, by means of ropes attached to the extremities of the spars in the sails, which are known by the name of a crowfoot; and thus the ship is tacked with very little trouble.

The prow, or head is, as usual with Chinese vessels, without stem; they are likewise without keel, and consequently make considerable leeway. The two anchors are made of a ponderous wood, called by the Chinese tye-mou, or iron wood, the several parts of which are strongly lashed and bolted together, and pointed with iron, though sometimes they carry large grapnels of four shanks. The arched roof of matting is the cabin, in which the seamen sleep, &c. and the bamboo spars on the quarter, are conveniently carried in that situation for the uses of the ship.

The several flags and ensigns are characteristic of the taste of the Chinese.

PORTRAIT OF CHOW-TA-ZHIN,

In his Dress of Ceremony.

CHOW-TA-ZHIN, a Quan, or Mandarin, holding a civil employment in the state, was, with Van-ta-zhin, entrusted by the Emperor with the care of the British Embassy during its residence in China. He was a man of grave deportment, strict integrity, and sound judgment, as well as of great erudition; having been preceptor to a part of the Imperial family.

His external honours were the customary distinction of a blue ball on his cap; from which was supended a peacock's feather, being a mark of additional rank.

He is attired in his full court dress, being a loose gown of silk or satin, covering an under vest richly embroidered in silk of the most vivid colours; the square badge on his breast, and its exact counterpart on the back, is also of rich embroidery, and contains the figure of an imaginary bird, which denotes the wearer to be a Mandarin of letters, in like manner as a tiger on the badge would shew the person to be in a military capacity. The beads worn round the neck are occasionally of coral, agate, or of perfumed wood, exquisitely carved, as affluence or fancy may dictate.

In his hand he holds a paper relative to the Embassy.

A CHINESE PORTER, OR CARRIER.

WHEN the wind is favourable, and where the level face of the country will admit, the Chinese sometimes hoist this simple kind of sail to lessen the exertion of the driver ; when the wind is adverse, the sail is laid aside, and another labourer employed to assist in pulling the machine, by means of a rope placed across his shoulders.

The carriage contains, among other articles, some vegetables, a basket of fruit, a box of tea, loose bamboos, and a jar of wine, the stopper of which is covered with clay, to prevent the air injuring the liquor ; on the side are placed his hat, and some implements for keeping the machine in order.

This contrivance is thus described by Milton, in his Paradise Lost, Book III. line 437, &c.

> " But in his way lights, on the barren plains
> " Of Sericana, where Chineses drive,
> " With sails and wind, their cany waggons light."

residence of the Embassy at Pekin, where one of the many edifices of that

THE HABITATION OF A MANDARIN.

THE house of a Mandarin is generally distinguished by two large poles erected before the gate; in the day-time flags are displayed on these poles as ensigns of his dignity, and during the night painted lanthorns are suspended on them.

The superior Chinese choose to live in great privacy, their habitations therefore are generally surrounded by a wall; their houses seldom exceed one story in height, though there are some few exceptions, as in the residence of the Embassy at Pekin, where one of the many edifices of that palace had apartments above the ground floor, and was occupied by the Secretary of Embassy.

The several rooms of a Chinese house are without ceilings, so that the timbers supporting the roof are exposed. The common articles of furniture are, frames covered with silk of various colours, adorned with moral sentences, written in characters of gold, which are hung in the compartments; on their tables are displayed curious dwarf trees, branches of agate, or gold and silver fish, all which are placed in handsome vessels of porcelain.

A MANDARIN'S TRAVELLING BOAT.

MANDARINS, who are employed in travelling from place to place on the public service, keep barges for that purpose, as carriages are kept in England.

They are generally ornamented by painting and varnishing the pannels and mouldings with various devices, &c. At night, or during rain, the part occupied by the Mandarin is inclosed by shutters, and the light is then received through lattices, covered with laminæ of oyster shells.

The gunwale of these barges (as with most Chinese vessels) is sufficiently broad for the watermen, &c. to pass from stem to stern, without inconvenience to passengers in the principal apartments.

The Mandarin is seen attended by soldiers and servants, who are bringing his dinner; the double umbrella, or ensign of his authority, is conspicuously placed to demand respect; the flag and board at the stern, with Chinese characters on them, exhibit his rank and employment; these insignia of power also serve as a signal for other vessels to make clear passage for him, in consequence of which, such boats are seldom obstructed in their progress through the immense number of vessels constantly employed on the canals. The master of any vessel who, by mismanagement, or even accident, should impede these officers in the exercise of their duty, would most likely receive the instant punishment of a certain number of blows from the bamboo, at the discretion of the Mandarin.

EARLY in the morning of the 30th of September, 1793, the Embassador and suite proceeded on their journey northward, to pay the customary compliment of meeting the Emperor, who was then returning from his summer residence in Tartary, to his palace at Pekin; on this occasion, each side of the road was lined, as far as the eye could reach, with mandarines, soldiers, &c. bearing banners, large silk triple umbrellas, and other insignia of Chinese royalty. The Print represents a soldier employed in bearing a standard, or gilt board, on which are depicted

A STANDARD BEARER.

EARLY in the morning of the 30th of September, 1793, the Embassador and suite proceeded on their journey northward, to pay the customary compliment of meeting the Emperor, who was then returning from his summer residence in Tartary, to his palace at Pekin; on this occasion, each side of the road was lined, as far as the eye could reach, with mandarines, soldiers, &c. bearing banners, large silk triple umbrellas, and other insignia of Chinese royalty. The Print represents a soldier employed in bearing a standard, or gilt board, on which are depicted characters, which probably display some title of the Emperor.

His dress is nankeen cotton, which is tied round the waist, with the imperial or yellow girdle, and his legs are cross-gartered: his hat is straw, neatly woven, and fastened under the chin; the crown is covered with a fringe of red silk, converging from the centre, where a feather is placed.

His sword, as is customary with the Chinese, is worn with the hilt behind.

A SACRIFICE AT THE TEMPLE.

THE Chinese have no regular sabbath, or fixed time for worshipping the Deity in congregation. Their temples being constantly open, are visited by the supplicants on every important undertaking, such as an intended marriage, the commencement of a long journey, building a house, &c.

The figure on the right hand is anxiously watching the fall of tallies, which he is shaking in a joint of bamboo; these are severally marked with certain characters, and as they fall, the characters are inserted by the priest in the book of fate. After the ceremony, the priest communicates to the votary the success of his prayers, which has been thus determined by lot.

The priesthood always shave the head entirely, and wear a loose dress of silk or nankeen, the colour of which is characteristic of their particular sect.

The figure kneeling before the sacred urn, in which perfumed matches are burning, is about to perform a sacrifice. On these occasions round pieces of gilt and silvered paper are burnt in tripods for that purpose, and at the same time quantities of crackers are discharged.

Behind the figures are seen two hideous idols. These statues are usually arranged against the walls of the temple, inclosed within a railing.

A SACRIFICE AT THE TEMPLE.

THE Chinese have no regular sabbath, or fixed time for worshipping the Deity in congregation. Their temples being constantly open, are visited by the supplicants on every important undertaking, such as an intended marriage, the commencement of a long journey, building a house, &c.

The figure on the right hand is anxiously watching the fall of tallies, which he is shaking in a joint of bamboo; these are severally marked with certain characters, and as they fall, the characters are inserted by the priest in the book of fate. After the ceremony, the priest communicates to the votary the success of his prayers, which has been thus determined by lot.

The priesthood always shave the head entirely, and wear a loose dress of silk or nankeen, the colour of which is characteristic of their particular sect.

The figure kneeling before the sacred urn, in which perfumed matches are burning, is about to perform a sacrifice. On these occasions round pieces of gilt and silvered paper are burnt in tripods for that purpose, and at the same time quantities of crackers are discharged.

Behind the figures are seen two hideous idols. These statues are usually arranged against the walls of the temple, inclosed within a railing.

Wm Alexander f.

A MILITARY STATION.

ALONG the canals and public roads of China, great numbers of military posts are erected, at which eight or ten soldiers are generally stationed.

Adjacent to each of these stands a look-out house, commanding an extensive prospect; and adjoining are placed five cones of plastered brick work, out of which certain combustibles are said to be fired in times of alarm from invasion or insurrection. In front of the building is a simple triumphal entrance, on which is an inscription suitable to the place. Near this the imperial ensign is elevated; and on the left of the house is a frame of wood, in which are deposited different arms, as pikes, matchlocks, bows, &c.

The vessel passing by with a double umbrella, contains some mandarin of distinction, who is saluted by the firing of three petards,* and by the guard, who are drawn out in a rank.

* The Chinese, on these occasions, never use more than three guns, which are always fired perpendicularly, to prevent accidents.

i. Alexander f.

A FISHING BOAT.

THIS Print illustrates a contrivance of the Chinese fishermen for raising their nets: the frame work is composed of that most useful plant the bamboo, which, uniting strength with lightness, is made use of on almost every occasion. When the weight of a man at the extremity of the lever is insufficient to lift a large draught of fish, he is assisted by a companion, as in the representation; the rest of the company are employed at dinner, steering, &c. protected from the sun and weather by a rude covering of mats: the boat is also provided with grapnels, and a lantern to prevent accidents at night. The distance is a view of the lake Poo-yang. On the left hand, near the benches, are some mounds of earth, which occur occasionally for several miles together; the purpose generally assigned to them is the repairing any accidental breach of the canal, with all possible expedition.

Another mode of fishing, often practised by the Chinese, is by means of a species of pelican, called the Leu-tze. See the Account of the British Embassy, by Sir George Staunton, Vol. II. p. 388.

A CHINESE COMEDIAN.

THEATRICAL exhibitions form one of the chief amusements of the Chinese: for though no public theatre is licensed by the government, yet every Mandarin of rank has a stage erected in his house, for the performance of dramas, and his visitors are generally entertained by actors hired for the purpose.

On occasions of public rejoicing, as the commencement of a new year, the birth-day of the Emperor, and other festivals, plays are openly performed in the streets, throughout the day, and the strolling players rewarded by the voluntary contributions of the spectators.

While the Embassador and his suite were at Canton, theatrical representations were regularly exhibited at dinner time, for their diversion. This character, which the Interpreter explained to be an enraged military officer, was, sketched from an actor performing his part before the embassy, December 19, 1793.

These entertainments are accompanied by music: during the peformance of which, sudden bursts, from the harshest wind instruments, and the sonorous gong, frequently stun the ears of the audience.

Females are not allowed to perform: their characters are therefore sustained by eunuchs; who, having their feet closely bandaged, are not easily distinguished from women.

The dresses worn by players, are those of ancient times.

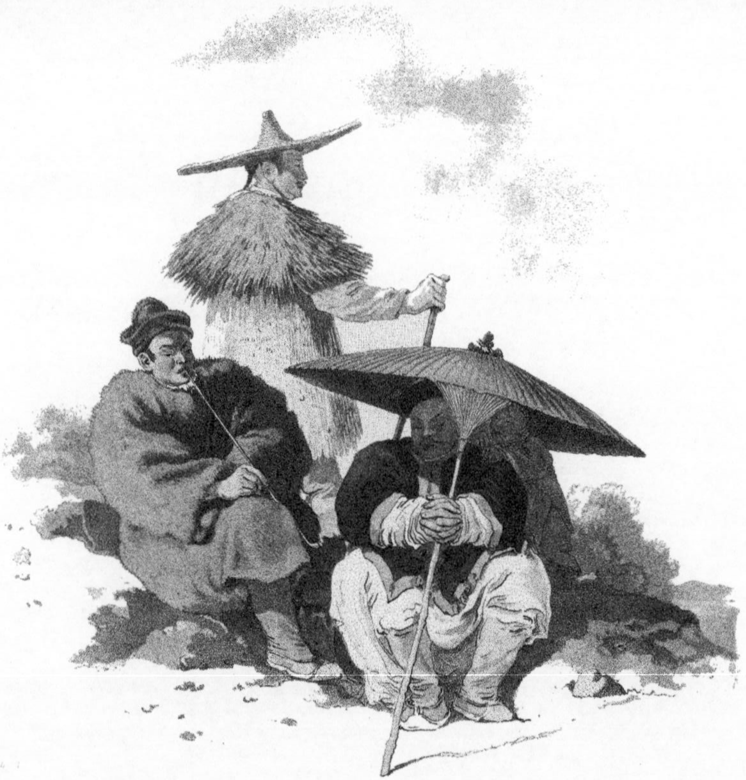

London Published Augt 12 1811 by G. and W. Nicol Pallmall

A GROUP OF CHINESE,

Habited for Rainy Weather.

DURING the rainy seasons, the natives of China wear an external dress, well calculated to keep them dry, and prevent, in a great measure, such diseases as arise from exposure to wet.

Watermen, peasantry, and others, employed in the open air, are generally provided with a coat made of straw, from which the rain runs off, as from the feathers of an aquatic bird: in addition to this, they sometimes wear a cloak, formed of the stalks of kow-liang (millet), which completely covers the shoulders; and a broad hat, composed of straw and split bamboo, which defends them both from sun and rain. A Chinese thus equipped (as in the standing figure,) may certainly defy the heaviest showers.

The soldier, under an umbrella of oiled canvas, wears his undress, consisting of a jacket of black nankeen, bordered with red: behind him is his child, to whom he is likewise affording shelter.

The figure smoaking, is habited in a large coat of skin, with the hair, or wool, remaining on it: sometimes the coat is turned, and the hairy side worn inwards.

A PAGODA, OR TEMPLE,

For religious Worship.

THE Chinese are scrupulously observant of moral and religious duties; and their country abounds with temples, of various forms, to which they resort, on every interesting occasion, and offer their sacrifices. Besides these temples, a small tabernacle, or niche, containing their household gods, is to be found in almost every house and ship.

Some religious ceremonies of the Chinese resemble those of the Church of Rome: and the Chinese Idol, denominated Shin-moo, is very similar to the representations of the Virgin and Child; both being figures of a female and an infant, with rays of glory issuing from their heads, and having lights burning before them, during the day as well as night.

The greater part of the people are of the sect of Fo; whose followers believe in the metempsychosis, and in a future state of happiness, after a virtuous life; and suppose, that the souls of the irreligious live hereafter in a state of suffering, and subject to the hardships endured by inferior animals.

The figures dressed in loose gowns are priests attending at the temple; and the back ground is a view of the city Tin-hai, Nov. 21, 1793.

London Published Aug.st 1st 1811 by J. and W. Neal, Edinburgh.

A SHIP OF WAR.

THE Chinese are so well supplied with the produce of their own country, as to require very little from distant lands; and it is to this native abundance the low state of navigation among them ought to be attributed.

Though they are said to have been acquainted with the use of the compass, from the earliest ages, yet they cannot be considered as expert seamen, either in their application of astronomy to nautical purposes, or skill in manœuvring their clumsy ships.

The compass is, however, an instrument venerated by the seaman, as a deity; and to which they sometimes offer sacrifices of flesh and fruit.

The drawing was made from a ship (Pin-gee-na) laying at anchor in the river, near Ning-po. These vessels may properly be termed floating garrisons; as they contain many soldiers, that are generally stationed near their principal towns.

These soldiers often hang their shields against the ship's quarter; and the rudder is lifted, by ropes, nearly out of the water, perhaps to preserve it while at anchor.

The ports are false; as few ships of the Chinese navy are, at present, supplied with artillery.

A SHIP OF WAR.

THE Chinese are so well supplied with the produce of their own country, as to require very little from distant lands ; and it is to this native abnndance the low state of navigation among them ought to be attributed.

Though they are said to have been acquainted with the use of the compass, from the earliest ages, yet they cannot be considered as expert seamen, either in their application of astronomy to nautical purposes, or skill in manœuvring their clumsy ships.

The compass is, however, an instrument venerated by the seaman, as a deity; and to which they sometimes offer sacrifices of flesh and fruit.

The drawing was made from a ship (Pin-gee-na) laying at anchor in the river, near Ning-po. These vessels may properly be termed floating garrisons: as they contain many soldiers, that are generally stationed near their principal towns.

These soldiers often hang their shields against the ship's quarter ; and the rudder is lifted, by ropes, nearly out of the water, perhaps to preserve it while at anchor.

The ports are false ; as few ships of the Chinese navy are, at present, supplied with artillery.

A SOLDIER IN HIS COMMON DRESS.

THE army of China cannot be considered formidable, their troops being naturally effeminate, and without the courage of European soldiers: one reason assigned for this is a mode of education which is not calculated to inspire a nation with courage, and it may partly be accounted for, from their having enjoyed uninterrupted peace since their subjugation by the Tartars.

Every soldier, on his marriage, and on the birth of a male child, is intitled to a donation from the Emperor; and the family of a deceased soldier receives likewise a gift of condolence.

The undress of a Chinese or Tartar soldier consists of a short jacket of black or red nankeen, with a border of another colour; under this is a garment of the same material, with long sleeves: when the weather is cold one or more dresses are worn under this. The flag at his back is of silk, and fastened by means of a socket attached behind; these are generally worn by every fifth man, and make a very gay appearance.

Their bows are of elastic wood, covered on the outside with a layer of horn, and require the power of from seventy to one hundred pounds in drawing them; the string is composed of silk threads closely woulded, and the arrows are well made and pointed with steel. Their scymeters, though rudely formed, are said to equal the best from Spain.

The military establishment of China, including cavalry and infantry, consists of 1,800,000 men. Vide the Appendix to Sir G. Staunton's Account of the Embassy to China.

THE PUNISHMENT OF THE BASTINADO

Is frequently used in China, for slight offences, and occasionally inflicted on all ranks.

When the number of blows sentenced by the Mandarin are few, it is considered as a gentle chastisement or fatherly correction, and when given in this mild way is not disgraceful, though the culprit is obliged, on his knees, with his forehead touching the ground, to thank the magistrate who so kindly ordered it to be administered.

Every Mandarin whose degree of nobility does not exceed the blue ball on his cap, is subject to this castigation, when ordered by his superior; but all above that rank can only be bastinadoed at the command of the Emperor.

The instrument used on these occasions is a split bamboo, several feet long, which is applied on the posteriors, and, in crimes of magnitude, with much severity. In petty offences, the offender (if he has the means) contrives dexterously to bribe the executioner, who, in proportion to the extent of the reward, mitigates the violence of the punishment, by laying the strokes on lightly, though with a feigned strength, to deceive the Mandarin; and it is said, that, for a douceur, some are ready to receive the punishment intended for the culprit; though, when eighty or a hundred blows is the sentence, it sometimes affects the life of the wretched criminal.

When a Mandarin is from home, he is generally attended by an officer of police, and perhaps one or more soldiers, who are ordered in this summary way to administer some half dozen blows on any careless person who might negligently omit the customary salute of dismounting his horse, or kneeling in the road before the great man as he passes by,

A PAI-LOU, OR TRIUMPHAL ARCH.

THESE monuments are erected for the purpose of transmitting the meritorious actions of good men to prosterity. Magistrates who have executed the duties of their high office with justice and integrity ; heroes who have signalized themselves in the field; and others of meaner station whose virtues or superior learning intitle them thereto, often receive this high honour, which likewise serves the purpose of exciting their posterity to the same virtuous actions.

These Pai-lous (usually translated, triumphal arches) are built at the public expense, generally with stone, though sometimes the better sort are made of marble, and some inferior ones of wood ; the chief of them have four uprights, each of one stone, which is often thirty feet in length ; horizontally across these are placed the transoms or friezes, on which the inscription is engraved with letters of gold, &c. and the summit of the fabric is crowned with projecting roofs richly ornamented.

This was drawn from one near the city of Ning-po, Nov. 17, 1793, where many others are erected, some of which were of a meaner kind, and had but two uprights. The inscription on this was thus translated by a Chinese attendant on the Embassy : " By the Emperor's supreme goodness, in the 59th year of Tchien-Lung, and on the first day, this triumphal edifice was erected in honour of Tchoung-ga-chung, the most high and learned Doctor of the Empire, and one of the Mandarins of the Tribunal of Arms."

VESSELS PASSING THROUGH A SLUICE.

THE imperial, or grand canal of China, extends, with little interruption from Canton, in lat. about 23° 15′, to Pekin in 39° 50′.

From this main trunk issue many branches, which pass through innumerable cities, towns, and villages, as roads through European countries; and by this means a communication is kept up with the utmost limits of the Empire; some lesser canals are also cut to counteract the overwhelming effects of inundation; these at the same time serve to convey superflous water over the low lands for the nutriment of rice, which requires immersion in water till it approaches maturity.

Locks and sluices of various kinds are therefore very numerous: the Print exhibits one chiefly designed as a bridge for the accommodation of foot passengers; the building on the right hand serves to shelter those who are employed in raising the bridge, as well as to preserve the stone under it, which records the name, &c. of the individual who was at the expense of its erection.

Some sluices are so constructed as to retain a considerable body of water for the use of vessels of greater draught; these have grooves cut in the masonry at the opposite piers, into which strong and heavy boards are dropped, similar to a portcullis, and when a sufficient quantity of water is collected, the planks are drawn up and the vessels pass through with considerable velocity, having previously paid a small toll for their admission through the sluice.

The vessel having the yellow or royal flag, is one inhabited by a part of the Embassy; some others occupied by the English have already passed through.

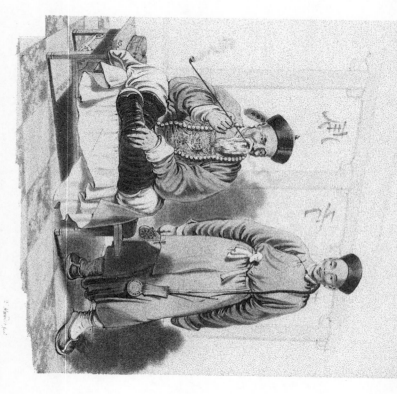

A MANDARIN

attended by a Domestic.

THOUGH chairs are commonly used in China, yet the Chinese sometimes choose to sit in the manner of the Turks.

This Mandarin, habited in his court attire, is one of the literati, and a civil magistrate, which is known by the bird embroidered in the badge on his breast: his high rank and honour are likewise denoted by the red ball and peacock's feather with three eyes attached to his cap, as also by the beads of pearl and coral appending from his neck; he is sitting in form on a cushion, smoking, and waiting the arrival of a visitor.

The servant bears in his hand a purse containing tobacco for his master; his girdle encloses a handkerchief, and from which also hangs his tobacco pouch and pipe. On the walls of the apartment Chinese characters are painted, signifying moral precepts.

A MANDARIN

attended by a Domestic.

THOUGH chairs are commonly used in China, yet the Chinese sometimes choose to sit in the manner of the Turks.

This Mandarin, habited in his court attire, is one of the literati, and a civil magistrate, which is known by the bird embroidered in the badge on his breast: his high rank and honour are likewise denoted by the red ball and peacock's feather with three eyes attached to his cap, as also by the beads of pearl and coral appending from his neck; he is sitting in form on a cushion, smoaking, and waiting the arrival of a visitor.

The servant bears in his hand a purse containing tobacco for his master; his girdle encloses a handkerchief, and from which also hangs his tobacco pouch and pipe. On the walls of the apartment Chinese characters are painted, signifying moral precepts.

sition and credulity among the unenlightended part of the people, who attribute every casual occurrence to the influence of some good or ill star, if the event forebode evil, they immediately repair to the proper idol with offerings, that the impending misfortune may be averted; if good, they also make sacrifices and return thanks.

These sacred edifices are commonly situated near the road side, or on the banks of canals for the convenience of travellers, &c. who are often observed prostrating before them; some are erected at the public expence, and dedicated to former Emperors, Mandarins, and others, for services rendered to their country; and some are built by charitable persons, to extend religious worship among the people.

On days of general rejoicing, as the commencement of the new year, new moon, Emperor ploughing the ground, feast of lanterns, &c. these buildings are much frequented, the people offering before the little gilt images inhabiting the fabric sacrifices of ready dressed animal food, fish, rice, and wine, in proportion to their ability or inclination; while innumerable crackers are fired, and a profusion of gilt paper and incense is burnt before the idol.

Sometimes a priest attends on such occasions to receive these offerings for the benefit of his fraternity, though more frequently the sacrifices of each suppliant are taken to his family and eaten as a feast. The buildings in the back ground are the residence of a Mandarin, known by the two flag staffs at the entrance: on the hill is a military station and a mutilated Pagoda, these being generally erected on an eminence.

A SMALL IDOL TEMPLE,

commonly called a Joss House.

THE general religion of China, Paganism, generates the grossest super-
stition and credulity among the unenlightended part of the people, who
attribute every casual occurrence to the influence of some good or ill
star; if the event forebode evil, they immediately repair to the proper
idol with offerings, that the impending misfortune may be averted; if
good, they also make sacrifices and return thanks.

These sacred edifices are commonly situated near the road side, or
on the banks of canals for the convenience of travellers, &c. who are
often observed prostrating before them; some are erected at the public
expence, and dedicated to former Emperors, Mandarins, and others, for
services rendered to their country; and some are built by charitable
persons, to extend religious worship among the people.

On days of general rejoicing, as the commencement of the new year,
new moon, Emperor ploughing the ground, feast of lanterns, &c. these
buildings are much frequented, the people offering before the little gilt
images inhabiting the fabric sacrifices of ready dressed animal food, fish,
rice, and wine, in proportion to their ability or inclination; while innumerable crackers are fired, and a profusion of gilt paper and incense
is burnt before the idol.

Sometimes a priest attends on such occasions to receive these offerings
for the benefit of his fraternity, though more frequently the sacrifices of
each suppliant are taken to his family and eaten as a feast. The buildings in the back ground are the residence of a Mandarin, known by the
two flag staffs at the entrance: on the hill is a military station and a
mutilated Pagoda, these being generally erected on an eminence.

best of our game-cocks. These battles, though tedious,
are countenanced and even praised by the Mandarins; and it is a
favourite diversion among the common in attendance of the palace, who
often hazard large sums in bets on the issue of a contest. If during a
conflict between these little foes, both sides should happen to fall
together, that which last endeavours to peck at his adversary, is deemed
the victor.

It is said, that oftentimes on the result of these battles, not only the
fortune, but even the wives and children of the parties wagering, are
put to the chance of being given up to the winner as concubines and
servants.

The figure smoking, holds in his hand some Chinese money threaded
on a string ; the man with a feather behind his cap is betting with him.

CHINESE GAMBLERS

with Fighting Quails.

It is more common in China to breed quails for fighting, than to bring up game-cocks, for the same purpose, in Europe. The male quails, descended from a good stock, are trained with great care; their owners teaching them to fight most furiously, and with a spirit equalling the best of our game-cocks. These battles, though forbidden by the laws, are countenanced and even practised by the Mandarins; and it is a favourite diversion among the eunuchs in attendance at the palace, who often hazard large sums in bets on the issue of a contest. If during a conflict between these little furies, both birds should happen to fall together, that which last endeavours to peck at his adversary, is deemed the victor.

It is said, that oftentimes on the result of these battles, not only the fortune, but even the wives and children of the parties wagering, are put to the chance of being given up to the winner as concubines and servants.

The figure smoking, holds in his hand some Chinese money threaded on a string; the man with a feather behind his cap is betting with him.

PORTRAITS OF SEA VESSELS,

generally called Junks.

On the 5th of August, 1793, the Embassador and his suite left the Lion and Hindostan, and embarked on board the brigs Clarence, Jackall, and Endeavour, when they immediately sailed for the Pay-ho, or White River, in the Gulph of Pe-tche-li : the other persons attached to the Embassy followed in Junks engaged for that purpose. These vessels, which also conveyed the presents for the Emperor, baggage, &c. are clumsily constructed, and carry about two hundred tons ; nevertheless, being flat-bottomed, they draw but little water, and are thereby enabled to cross the shallows at the entrances of the Chinese rivers.

These Junks are of the same form at stem and stern, and the hold is divided into compartments, each being water-tight : the masts are of one tree, and very large : their main and fore sails are of matting, composed of split bamboos and reeds interwoven together ; the mizen sails are of nankeen cloth.

The rudders, (which are generally lifted out of the water when at anchor,) are rudely formed, and cannot be worked with dexterity ; the steering compasses are placed near them, and surrounded with perfumed matches.

The anchor of four points is of iron, the other of wood ; at the quarters are stowed some bamboo spars ; and these junks are gaudily adorned with ensigns, vanes, &c. agreeably to the Chinese taste.

PORTRAITS OF SEA VESSELS,

generally called Junks.

ON the 5th of August, 1793, the Embassador and his suite left the Lion and Hindostan, and embarked on board the brigs Clarence, Jackall, and Endeavour, when they immediately sailed for the Pay-ho, or White River, in the Gulph of Pe-tchi-li: the other persons attached to the Embassy followed in Junks engaged for that purpose. These vessels, which also conveyed the presents for the Emperor, baggage, &c. are clumsily constructed, and carry about two hundred tons; nevertheless, being flat-bottomed, they draw but little water, and are thereby enabled to cross the shallows at the entrances of the Chinese rivers.

These Junks are of the same form at stem and stern, and the hold is divided into compartments, each being water-tight: the masts are of one tree, and very large; their main and fore sails are of matting, composed of split bamboos and reeds interwoven together; the mizen sails are of nankeen cloth.

The rudders, (which are generally lifted out of the water when at anchor,) are rudely formed, and cannot be worked with dexterity; the steering compasses are placed near them, and surrounded with perfumed matches.

The anchor of four points is of iron, the other of wood; at the quarters are stowed some bamboo spars; and these junks are gaudily adorned with ensigns, vanes, &c. agreeably to the Chinese taste.

London Published Jan. 1st 1804 by W. Miller Old Bond Street.

A SOLDIER OF CHU-SAN,

Armed with a Matchlock Gun, &c.

THE Chinese are supposed to have known the use of fire-arms and gunpowder at a very early period, but since the conquest of that country by the Tartars, the chief expenditure of gunpowder has been in the frequent practice of firing salutes and discharging of fireworks: in the ingenious contrivance of the latter they are eminently skilful.

The army of China is at present very ill disciplined; its strength consists only in its numbers, which would not compensate in the day of battle for their ignorance of military tactics, and want of personal courage.

The general dress of the soldiery is cumbrous, and for the southern provinces almost suffocating, being lined and quilted. At the right side of this figure hangs his cartouch-box, and on the left his sword, with the point forwards. The matchlock is of the rudest workmanship, and has a forked rest near the muzzle.

It must be thought extraordinary that the Chinese government should continue the use of this clumsy weapon, when the ingenuity of the people so well enables them to manufacture muskets equal to those of Europe.

In the back-ground is a military post, having the usual number of soldiers attending it; these are called out by the sentinel on the tower, who is beating a gong, to announce the approach of a man of rank, who is entitled to the compliment of a military salute.

A SOLDIER OF CHU-SAN,

Armed with a Matchlock Gun, &c.

THE Chinese are supposed to have known the use of fire-arms and gun-powder at a very early period, but since the conquest of that country by the Tartars, the chief expenditure of gunpowder has been in the frequent practice of firing salutes and discharging of fireworks: in the ingenious contrivance of the latter they are eminently skilful.

The army of China is at present very ill disciplined; its strength consists only in its numbers, which would not compensate in the day of battle for their ignorance of military tactics, and want of personal courage.

The general dress of the soldiery is cumbrous, and for the southern provinces almost suffocating, being lined and quilted. At the right side of this figure hangs his cartouch-box, and on the left his sword, with the point forwards. The matchlock is of the rudest workmanship, and has a forked rest near the muzzle.

It must be thought extraordinary that the Chinese government should continue the use of this clumsy weapon, when the ingenuity of the people so well enables them to manufacture muskets equal to those of Europe.

In the back-ground is a military post, having the usual number of sol-diers attending it; these are called out by the centinel on the tower, who is beating a gong, to announce the approach of a man of rank, who is entitled to the compliment of a military salute.

London Published Jan.r 1.st 1804 by W. Miller Old Bond Street.

EXAMINATION OF A CULPRIT

Before a Mandarin.

This subject represents a female, charged with prostitution. Such an offence is generally punished by the bamboo.

EXAMINATION OF A CULPRIT

Before a Mandarin.

Tʜɪs subject represents a Female, charged with prostitution. Such an offender is generally punished publicly, by numerous blows with the pan-tsee, or bamboo; and, in cases of notorious infamy, is doomed to suffer the additional sentence of bearing the can-gue; sometimes, however, corporal punishment is commuted into a pecuniary fine.

The Magistrate, habited in full dress, is known to be of royal blood, by the circular badge on his breast, that worn by every other Mandarin being square. The Secretary, who is taking minutes of the proceedings, wears on his girdle his handkerchief and purses, together with a case containing his knife and chopsticks. These purses are merely for ornament, not being made to open.

The Chinese write with a hair pencil and Indian ink: the pencil is held vertically, and the letters are arranged in perpendicular lines from the top of the page to the bottom, beginning at the right and ending on the left side of the paper. The cap worn by the officer of police is distinguished by certain letters which denote the name of the Mandarin he serves.

The manner in which the prisoner is presented is characteristic of the insolence of office and harshness which (even female) delinquents are subject to in that country.

VIEW AT YANG-TCHEOU,

In the Province of Che-kian.

The city of Yang-tcheou (through which the Embassy passed on the 4th of November, 1793), is of the second order, which is known by its termination, *tcheou.*

The chief building in this subject is a sacred Temple, having the two characteristic flags : on the right is seen a monument, a fort, and part of the city walls.

Chinese fortifications are generally constructed in a manner which Europeans would not consider formidable, but they are, nevertheless, proportional to the efforts of the probable assailants, it being more likely they would be employed against the natives in civil warfare, than against a foreign enemy.

On the fore-ground is seen a tower, and another part of the walls. These defences are in some places continued without interruption over the rivers and canals, and thus become fortified bridges. On the last-mentioned tower and wall are soldiers presenting their shields in front of the embrasures, in compliment to the Embassador. This singular mode of salute, when continued along an extensive line of wall, produced an interesting effect.

On the river are seen many travelling vessels, &c. ; the nearest was occupied by a Mandarin attending the Embassy.

London Published Jan.ᵗ 1ˢᵗ 1804 by W. Miller Old Bond Street.

TEMPORARY BUILDING AT TIEN-SIN,

Erected for the Reception of the Embassador.

On the 13th of October, 1793, the Embassy reached Tien-sin, being then on its route towards Canton.

This building of mats (on the banks of the Un-leang), was constructed by order of the chief Mandarin of the city, for the purpose of complimenting the Embassador, and entertaining him and his suite with refreshments, &c.

The landing-place was decorated with mats, fancifully painted; the chief Magistrate of the district sat in a chair, while the inferior Mandarins stood in a rank on each side to receive his Lordship, had he thought proper to accept it.

The entertainment consisted of a profusion of poultry, confectionary, fresh fruits, preserves, jars of wine, &c. &c. all which were distributed among the various barges of the Embassy, which are distinguished by

TEMPORARY BUILDING AT TIEN-SIN,

Erected for the Reception of the Embassador.

On the 13th of October, 1793, the Embassy reached Tien-sin, being then on its route towards Canton.

This building of mats (on the banks of the Un-leang), was constructed by order of the chief Mandarin of the city, for the purpose of complimenting the Embassador, and entertaining him and his suite with refreshments, &c.

The landing-place was decorated with mats, fancifully painted; the chief Magistrate of the district sat in a chair, while the inferior Mandarins stood in a rank on each side to receive his Lordship, had he thought proper to debark.

The entertainment consisted of a profusion of poultry, confectionary, fresh fruits, preserves, jars of wine, &c. &c. all which were distributed among the various barges of the Embassy, which are distinguished by their yellow flags.

London. Published Nov.r 1.st by W. Miller Old Bond Street.

W. Alexander delt.

A TRADESMAN.

THE dress worn by this person is common among the middle class of the people. The jacket without sleeves is of silk, having a collar made from slips of velvet; the stockings are of cotton quilted, with a border of the same, and his shoes are embroidered.

His pipe, pouch, knife, and chopsticks are suspended from a sash; in his right hand is a basket of birds' nests, which he carries for sale to the epicures of China.

These nests are constructed by birds of the swallow kind, and appear to be composed of the fine filaments of certain sea-weeds, cemented together with a gelatinous substance collected from the rocks and stones on the sea-shore. They are chiefly found in caverns on the islands near the Straits of Sunda, and on an extensive cluster of rocks and islands, called the Paracels, on the coast of Cochin-China.

These nests, when dissolved in water, become a thick jelly, which to a Chinese taste has a most delicious flavour, and communicates, in their opinion, an agreeable taste to whatever food it is combined with. They are therefore highly prized by the upper ranks, and their great expence excludes their use among the poor.

On the bank near which he stands, is a post to which a lantern is attached; the back ground is a scene at Han-tcheou-foo.

London Published Nov.r 1.st 1804 by W. Miller Old Bond Street.

A FUNERAL PROCESSION.

THE leader of this solemn pageant is a priest, who carries a lighted match, with tin-foil and crackers, to which he sets fire when passing a temple or other building for sacred purposes. Four musicians with gongs, flutes, and trumpets follow next; then comes two persons with banners of variegated silk, on the tops of which two lanterns are suspended; these are followed by two mourners clad in loose gowns, and caps of coarse canvas; next to these is the nearest relative, overwhelmed with grief, dressed in the same humble garments, and is prevented from tearing his dishevelled hair by two supporters, who affect to have much ado to keep the frantic mourner from laying violent hands on himself; then follows the corpse, in an uncovered coffin, of very thick wood varnished, on which a tray is placed, containing some viands as offerings; over the coffin is a gay ornamented canopy carried by four men; and lastly, in an open carriage, three females with dejected countenances, arrayed in white, their hair loose, and fillets across their foreheads.

Contrary to European ideas, which comsider white as the symbol of joy, and use it at nuptial celebrations, it is in China the emblem of mourning, and expressive of sorrow.

The scene is at Macao: in the fore ground is a large stone with a monumental inscription; in the distance is seen the inner harbour, and the flag staves of a bonzes' temple.

W. Alexander fecit

London Published Nov.ʳ 1.ˢᵗ 1814 by W.ᵐ Miller Old Bond Street

A STONE BUILDING

in the Form of a Vessel.

In one of the courts of the hotel, appointed for the residence of the Embassador in Pekin, was an edifice representing a covered barge ; the hull was of hewn stone, situated in a hollow or pond that was filled with water, which was supplied from time to time by buckets from a neighbouring well, as might be necessary ; the upper part of this whimsical building was used by part of the suite of the Embassy as a dining room.

The fragments of rocks artificially piled on each other with flowerpots, containing dwarf trees here and there interspersed, will convey in some degree an idea of Chinese taste in ornamental gardening on a small scale.

Over the roof of the stone vessel, and above the wall enclosing this extensive mansion, the tops of a few pagodas, a triumphal arch, and other public buildings were visible within the walls of the great city of Pekin.

This great mansion was built by a late (Hoppo or) collector of customs at Canton, from which situation he was promoted to the collectorship of salt duties at Tien-sien ; but his frauds and extortions being here detected, the whole of his immense wealth was confiscated to the crown.

A FISHERMAN AND HIS FAMILY,

regaling in their Boat.

THE female of the group, surrounded by her children, is smoking her pipe. One of these has a gourd fastened to its shoulders, intended to preserve it from drowning, in the event of its falling overboard.

The whole family sleep under the circular mats, which also serve as a cover to retreat to in bad weather; through the roof is a pole, surmounted by a lantern, and on the flag are depicted some Chinese characters.

On the gunwale are three of the leutze, or fishing corvorants of China; in size, they are nearly as large as the goose, and are very strongly formed both in their beak, their legs, and webbed feet. On the lakes of China, immense numbers of rafts and small boats are frequently seen employed in this kind of fishery. A well-trained bird, at a signal from its master, immediately plunges into the water, and soon returns with its prey to the boat to which it belongs; sometimes it encounters a larger fish than it can well manage, in which case the owner goes to assist in the capture; it is said indeed, that these birds have the sagacity to help each other.

That the young leutzes may not gorge their prey, a ring is put on their neck to prevent its passing into the stomach; when they have taken enough to satisfy their master the ring is taken off, and they are then allowed to fish for themselves.

Beyond the boat is a sluice, or flood-gate, for the passage of vessels. The distances behind indicate the serpentine direction of the canal.

I N D E X.

INDEX.

Printed by W. Bulmer and Co,
Cleveland-row, St. James's,

COSTUME OF GREAT BRITAIN,

IN A SERIES OF COLOURED ENGRAVINGS.

THE SUBJECTS COLLECTED, ARRANGED, AND EXECUTED, AND THE
DESCRIPTIONS WRITTEN BY

W. H. PYNE.

PUBLISHED BY WILLIAM MILLER, ALBEMARLE STREET,

(REMOVED FROM OLD BOND-STREET.)

THE Work will be composed of Characters, most of whom are peculiar to this Country, forming a
selection of Persons whose Habits, Customs, Employments, and Dress, distinguish them from the
great mass of the people.

Within the last half century a striking change has taken place in this Kingdom, by blending
almost all external distinctions in the different orders of Society. The Nobleman is seldom known
by his star, nor is the Physician or Lawyer discovered by the bag wig, the cut of the coat, or the cane;
and had Hogarth painted his subjects at this period, his works would have lost a considerable share
of their interest; for the peculiarities of dress were often accompanied by singularity of manner;
and those representations which we see upon the Stage, are but slight exaggerations upon the manners of the people at the beginning of the last century; indeed such is the effect given by the aid of
Dress, that certain characters in modern comedy are represented in the Costume of our great grand-
fathers. But the Figures introduced into this Work will owe a great portion of their character to
the Pictoresqueness of their Dress, being selected from such Institutions, Manufactories, or Establishments, as have preserved their habits even for centuries; and it is presumed that GREAT BRITAIN
offers as much interesting subject for a Costume as any country in Europe. Each Character will be
drawn from life, and every minutiæ of Dress, and the Implements and Appendages to their different
Employments, with the Badges of their various Offices, will be attended to with the most scrupulous
exactness. In short, the Work here offered to the Public will form a correct ENGLISH COSTUME
of the PRESENT AGE.

CONDITIONS.

THE Work will be printed at the Press of W. BULMER and Co. on Imperial Quarto Paper (uniform with the
COSTUMES OF CHINA, TURKEY, RUSSIA, and AUSTRIA,) and will consist of Twelve Numbers, at Fifteen
Shillings each. A Number will contain Five Engravings, coloured exactly to represent the Original Drawings, and
accompanied with Ten Pages of Letter Press, describing the Origin, Regulations, and Customs, &c. of each Subject,
with the Institutions, Establishments, Manufactories, &c. to which they severally belong, forming a great variety of
interesting matter; the whole being written from Original Documents collected expressly for this Work.

The First Number will be published the first day of January next, and a Number will certainly be published
every three Months.

WS - #0026 - 200824 - C0 - 229/152/16 [18] - CB - 9780331591873 - Gloss Lamination